ON MY WAY TO BECOMING A MAN

ON MY WAY TO BECOMING A MAN

A. D. Winans

Books™

The New York Quarterly Foundation, Inc.
New York, New York

NYQ Books™ is an imprint of The New York Quarterly Foundation, Inc.

The New York Quarterly Foundation, Inc.
P. O. Box 2015
Old Chelsea Station
New York, NY 10113

www.nyq.org

Copyright © 2014 by A. D. Winans

All rights reserved. No part of this book may be used or reproduced in any manner whatsoever without written permission of the author except in the case of brief quotations embodied in critical articles and reviews.

First Edition

Set in New Baskerville

Layout by Joseph Hamersly
Cover Design by Raymond P. Hammond

Cover art: "The Grand Review"; 48" X 96"; oil on canvas; 1990-1991
 by Frank Wright; used with kind permission of the artist

Digital cover image graciously provided by Mark Gulezian

Author photo by Alexsey Dayen

Library of Congress Control Number: 2014934950

ISBN: 978-1-935520-25-2

ON MY WAY TO BECOMING A MAN

Acknowledgements

The author wishes to express his regrets for not being able to name individual magazines that originally published some of the poems found in this book. Due to a fire at his apartment, the credit list, among other things, was destroyed.

The credits listed here are for book publishers that subsequently published many of the poems appearing in this book:

Black Bear, BOS Press, Erbacee, Fallen Angel, Green Bean Press, French Bread Publications, Integrity Times Press, Little Red Tree Publishing, Propaganda Press, Presa Press, Second Coming, and Yee Olde Font Shoppe.

Contents

ON MY WAY TO BECOMING A MAN /*11*
LACKLAND AIR FORCE BASE /*13*
LACKLAND AIR FORCE BASE TWO /*14*
LACKLAND AIR FORCE BASE THREE /*16*
LACKLAND AIR FORCE BASE FOUR /*18*
PANAMA I /*19*
PANAMA II /*20*
PANAMA III /*21*
PANAMA IV /*22*
RETURNING HOME FROM PAMAMA /*23*
AMERICA /*24*
GROWING UP IN AMERICA /*28*
THE SYSTEM /*30*
THE BALLAD OF GENERAL YAMASHITA /*32*
VIETNAM ERA POEM /*34*
POLITICS /*35*
POEM FOR RONALD REAGAN /*36*
REAGANITES /*38*
DIAL 890 REMEMBERING THE GOOD OLD SIXTIES /*41*
FOR CHARLES OLCOTT /*43*
LIES /*45*
DURING THE DEBATE BETWEEN CLINTON AND DOLE /*47*
THEY'RE AT IT AGAIN /*49*
CHINATOWN SWEAT SHOP /*51*
FACTORY WORKER /*52*
LOSS OF INNOCENCE /*53*
ON THE BOMBING OF YUGOSLAVIA /*54*
I WILL NOT PLEDGE ALLEGIANCE /*55*
WE THE PEOPLE /*56*

BILL /57
OLD JOE /58
FOLSOM PRISON /59
SAN QUENTIN PRISON /60
UNTITLED /61
POEM FOR HIS HOLINESS /62
SITTING BULL /63
POEM FOR THE GOVERNOR OF ARIZONA /64
222 EDDY STREET /65
4 A.M. INSOMNIA POEM /66
SAN FRANCISCO BLUES /68
LOOKING FOR AN ANSWER /70
ON WHY I WRITE POLITICAL POEMS /73
POEM FOR ALLEN GINSBERG /75
HOSPITAL POEM /77
THE OLD POETS /80
THE SHOW MUST GO ON /82
POEM FOR A POET FRIEND /92
DANCING WITH WORDS /96
FOURTH OF JULY POEM /98
POEM FOR ROBERTO VARGAS AND THE NICARAGUAN
   FREEDOM FIGHTERS /101
I AM SAN FRANCISCO /104

ON MY WAY TO BECOMING A MAN

ON MY WAY TO BECOMING A MAN

on my way to Lackland Air Force Base
the train stopped to take on passengers
giving me the chance to get off
stretch my legs and relieve myself

on returning from the men's room
an elderly black man approached me
wanting to know where the bathroom was
and when I pointed in the direction
of where I had just come from
he nervously shuffled his feet
and said: "No, the colored room"
and being naive and from the North
I had no idea what he was talking about
when suddenly a woman came running
out from behind a concession stand
her face red with anger
yelling for the old man
to leave me alone
as I tried in vain to calm her down
telling her it was all right
he was only looking for the men's room

"that boy knows where
the colored room is"
she said, shooing the old man away
as I boarded the train
turning to see him bent over
"a colored only" water fountain
as the train picked up steam
sparks flying from the tracks
taking me on my way
to becoming a man
where I would have my serial number

branded into my head
and made to wear dog tags
around
my neck
to remind me I was the property
of Uncle Sam

LACKLAND AIR FORCE BASE

during basic training
the DI took us on a field exercise
bagged a rabbit
took out his survival knife
and slit it up the middle
sliding his hand inside
and coming out with its guts
then drank of the blood
smiling as he said:
"it makes a man of you."
two three others jumped right in
as others screamed in joy or agony
one leaving his breakfast
on the ground

we wore the smell of death
like a whore's sweet perfume
the day we graduated
with company honors
at the base parade ground
the DI grinning ear to ear

LACKLAND AIR FORCE BASE TWO

at Lackland Air Force Base
during basic training
we were given a survey
to fill out
and asked some questions
by the DI
about our religious affiliation

when the sergeant asked me
what religion I was
I answered Protestant
and when he asked what denomination
I was
I answered Protestant
not having practiced religion that much

the sergeant didn't like my response
I think he thought
I was a wise-ass
he asked again what denomination I was
and I responded in a like manner
until I found myself taken
to the company barracks
by a pimply-faced corporal
with a demented smile on his face

once there I was made to strip down
to my shorts
and ordered to sit down
on a straight-back chair
while the two men proceeded
to use me for batting practice
asking the same damn question
over and over again

once there I was made
to strip down my shorts
until they grew tired of the game
and told me I could get dressed
that they would put down atheist
and why didn't I just say so
in the first place
and save everyone the trouble

LACKLAND AIR FORCE BASE THREE

at Lackland Air Force Base
in San Antonio Texas
the DI put us in formation
and introduced himself to us
one fat boy
he called Porky Pig
and gave him a shot to the gut
and said to another dude:
"how did the food taste?"
and the dude answered
"good sir."
and the DI punched him too
and said,
"you're a liar
it tasted like shit,
didn't it?"
and the kid tried hard
not to cry and said,
"yes sir."
and the DI said,
"how in the hell do you know?
are you a shit eater?"
and the boy said,
"no sir."
and the DI said,
"well I think you are."
and told the corporal
to take down his name
they'd get back to him later

this kind of abuse went on
week after week
and on the final week
when we graduated
I learned that the DI

had served in Korea
and was a decorated hero
in town
he said his job was
to make men of us
raising his drink
and toasting to us
but when you looked him
in the eyes
it was like seeing a tombstone
staring back at you
and that boot camp speech
was like a death charm
I will carry with me
to my grave

LACKLAND AIR FORCE BASE FOUR

the DI gathered us around
and told us that
the Korean War was not over
the truce notwithstanding
said the Godless Commies
had no code of honor
and could not be trusted
to keep their word
so they separated some of us
myself included
and assigned us to the elite
Air Base Defense school
taught by hardened ex-marines
one kid was weaker than
the rest of us
worse yet he was a pacifist
they took him out on the rifle range
stripped him down to his shorts
and had him shoot at targets
for hours in the rain

a week later
he came down with pneumonia
spent two weeks in the base hospital
and was later dropped from the school
the military intelligence boys questioned
us for days on end
but no one betrayed
the code of honor
for we were taught to obey
and honor was second only
to the kill

PANAMA I

in Panama City
the day they killed
the President
a group of us were given rifles
and a loaded clip
and told to assist
the Panama National Guard
in whatever manner we could
like rousting civilians
who might be possible assassins

we split off from
the rest of them
six of us
four half-drunk
and one stoned on grass
and dumb ass me wanting
to be anywhere but there
when we came across this woman
working in the fields

and what started off as questioning
turned out to be a strip search
eager hands violating
every part of her body
and when I protested
I was told to shut up
or get with it

they laughed
they were only looking
for concealed weapons
wrestling her to the ground
as I walked away in shame
not wanting to be part of what
I had no chance of stopping

PAMAMA II

1955
the President of Panama
gunned down at the racetrack
for having the courage
to build schools and roads
for thinking of the people

elite unit troops issued guns
and sent to town
to roust civilians
in the street
and keep order

two hours into forced insanity
I sneak off to the Amigo Bar
to smoke a joint in silence
trying to shut out the madness
until I'm oblivious
to what is happening outside
half the men looking
for an assassin
the other half too stoned to care

the sweet smell of Mary Jane
floats through the air
filling the bar
as I put on the safety
and lay my rifle to one side
smiling at the bar girl
on the other side of the bar
not knowing whether
she would like
to make love to me
or put a bullet
in my head

PANAMA III

I volunteer for every
war zone there is
wanting out of this
fucking jungle
but I guess
I'm too important

tonight I'm assigned to guard
the President's airplane
and you can see
he's in trouble
from the locks and chains
they have around
his icebox
and further down the runway
troops with machine guns
sit behind sandbags

I listen to their laughter
muffled from the distance
my mind replaying images
of that young woman stripped
and raped while the President
dines in splendor
at the U.S. Embassy

PANAMA IV

Panama City could
have been any slum city
in America
run by corrupt police
and politicians
but when you add
the American Troops
sent there to safeguard
the people
it was worse than any slum
you might imagine

shacks for homes
naked children playing
in the street
twelve-year-old boys
selling pictures of naked women
being fucked by dogs
or selling their young sisters
to the highest bidder

taxi drivers taking you
to the famed donkey show
or to the homes
of young whores while
less than ten miles away
in the American Canal Zone
it's hometown U. S. A.
the Governor's ball
U.S. civilian police
and white-skinned women
sipping coffee and tea
Armed Forces TV selling
the American dream

RETURNING HOME FROM PAMAMA

they had this bar
at Ocean Beach called
the Chalet
it used to be a hangout for vets
the American Legion boys
most of them fat and balding
the years piling up like litter
one so old
he claimed he was gassed in
W.W. I
you never knew whether
to believe him or not
he just sat there staring
talking into his beer
humming a song:
"over here. over there."
and using terms
like dough boy and pill box
and you just somehow
knew he had to have been there
was still there would always
be there

AMERICA

drummed out of the infantry of death
I came back to you carrying
the poems of my soul
opened the door of life
and found only death inside

America
I have read the state of the union
and listened to the state of the economy
by statesmen in a state of hysteria

America where the poor and the black
are sentenced to Attica
and the rich serve time
in the halls of Congress

America where
the coal miner's lungs are used
for corporate profit in between
funerals for preventable mine deaths
America where the only sound heard
is the opening and closing
of the downtown Bank of America

America where the angry voices
of soccer moms can be heard
preparing their children for death
amidst the hurried jerks of masturbation
coming from the closets of the university

America where the elderly
are treated like abandoned railroad boxcars
kept idle unemployed
forced to walk the streets
like an unacceptable poem

America
It's hard living in a country where
the hours are shaped like coffins
the law and order administration
running wild at Waco and Ruby Ridge

America where the politicians sold
the country to General Motors and IBM
and gave the people buffalo stew
and scientology

Reader's Digest has renewed its option
on the educational system
the mafia weans the poor on drugs
while McDonald's and Coca Cola
compete for the nation's heart

America
you leave a trail of death behind
everywhere you go
desecrating the bodies of men
women and children
from Wounded Knee to Vietnam
from Iran to Afghanistan
you leave behind a trail of genocide
as your calling card

America where the Narcs
of New York City
grow fat on the fears of thousands
of junkies
where the high priest of the cemetery
drinks the rooster's blood
at the crossroad of reality

America
where holiness is found
in the bowels of Buddha
where Christ died on the cross
and the police were quick
to take his place

America
the years grow heavy
in the cavity of my heart
leaving me feeling
like an army mule carrying
a cargo of death
your bloodstained message
ringing loud and clear
in every cash register across America
the American way
if you can't kill them
buy them into the system

America
I grow older carrying a new found vision
more warm than a child's smile
walking the streets of my mind's third eye
lady death blinking like
the flickering candles on a birthday cake

America
you are the only country I have known
for any length of time
and unlike some poets
I have no desire for Cuba or Moscow
but I am a man. I am a poet.
I am the energy running through
your withered veins

not afraid of your shock and awe
your disregard for international law
all too aware of the storm troopers of justice
who would turn off the beauty
and discard it like a rusted faucet

these men in blue
who sniff the blood of my wounds
like a hound dog crossing a river of blood
their sirens playing mad tunes outside my window
like a poet forced to read underwater
where the poet twice dead and once resurrected
turns over in his grave
but the middle finger he raises
is jammed back down his throat
until the shit he shits is theirs
and the blood they bleed is his
and the cries united fill the sky
like a lonely bird lost in flight

GROWING UP IN AMERICA

as a child
I thrilled at the railroad trains
riding out of the badlands
not knowing they were owned
by robber barons

I watched the Cavalry charge
the Indian villages
like Attila the Hun
believing Custer a hero
and Sitting Bull a savage
not taught in school about
the deadly smallpox plague
diseased blankets traded Indians
for title to their land
a deadly plot to murder
an entire nation

generations of ripped-off cultures
gather in the museum of history
dolphins die in tuna fishermen's nets
while pelican eggs refuse to hatch
victim of man's greed and waste
as the blistered hands
of faceless migrant workers
reach out for recognition
only to find death in pesticide-
laced foods
the tools of revolution
laid aside rusting
from affluence
and false security

the dreams of thousands
of brave warriors
lay buried in unmarked graves
no historical monument
will make mention of them
no history book will tell the truth
their children buried
in graves so small
their parents wear their memories
like an anchor weighed
to the tip of their tongues

THE SYSTEM

there are old men and women
who have worked all their life
who have put in thirty-five
forty years for the right
to a pension
only to be laid off
and given a two-week
severance package
abandoned left to a living
at half the pay

there are old people
who have worked
most of their lives
only to witness the company
go belly-up
and find there is no pension
fund left

you can find them on park benches
or wandering lonely supermarkets
or sitting daily at neighborhood bars
nursing their drinks
like a blood transfusion

they come in different flavors
like lifesavers
some thin and balding
some fat and sweating
some complaining bitterly
some too proud
to let the pain show

trapped by false promises
trapped by a belief
in a system that has abandoned
them

for the most part
they suffer in silence
and go unnoticed
to be carted off
by a coroner
who sees them
as morning cereal
going about his business
thinking about dinner
thinking about a glass of wine
thinking how it used to be
how it should be
how it might have been

it's the way of life
it's the way of rats and mice
it's the system where
just staying alive becomes
a small victory

THE BALLAD OF GENERAL YAMASHITA

they tried the tiger of Malaysia
in a theater banquet room
converted into a makeshift
courthouse
convened a five general
board of inquiry
none of whom held
a law degree
but then this wasn't
an issue here

General Yamashita responsible
for atrocities of naval forces
only forty-eight hours under
his control
in command only one month
before its total collapse
cut off from his troops
and all means of communication

the trial lasted two days
the verdict hurried
to coincide with the anniversary
of Pearl Harbor

found guilty by a prosecution
team of five former
district attorneys
and sentenced to death by hanging
the Supreme Court upholding
the verdict

General Yamashita
President Truman knew
the horror of Hiroshima
but the losers do not try
the victors

General Yamashita
you should have known
justice is a circus
with a ring master
wielding a heavy whip

you standing tall
facing that tribunal
on a hot Philippine afternoon
eyes clear skin wrinkled
asking the court for no mercy
knowing none would come
your way

lady justice's knuckles
crack harshly in the night
witness to a dying land
where law students study briefs
in disbelief and angry ghosts
of justice show no grief

VIETNAM ERA POEM

tuned in the television set
down the hall
and turned on the society ball
ticker tape parade for moon men
broadway go-go girls doing the swim
burned children crying in my ear
vice president playing on my fears
facts and figures
and more government lies
another commercial
another young boy dies
heroism found in Vietnam fields
hospital costs rising according
to Blue Shield

flowers grow and bloom
funeral horses strangle
on gargoyle plumes
baby crying in the background
head so fucked-up
can't make a sound
latest love lies naked
in upstairs bed
only one God Damn thing
going on inside her head

POLITICS

going to be a Reagan stamp
one of these days
the old man tells me
at Gino and Carlo's Bar
in between my second
and third drinks

you can't beat these
damn politicians
he says
but Reagan will be patient
he's going to be a stamp
one of these days
perforated holes in between
the spaces on each sheet
guess that's the only way
to lick the son-of-a-bitch

POEM FOR RONALD REAGAN

Reagan appears
on the Capitol steps
his mind wanders back
to Hollywood U.S.A.
his eyes blink like
a pinball machine
his lips move in puppet
like precision

the White House staff passes by
they are dressed in crisp uniforms
goose-stepping along
with flags raised high
in the sky

Nancy Reagan appears
on the balcony
she is dressed up to look
like Shirley Temple
as she waves to the cheering
courtesans engaged in conversation
with the Pope

below in the courtyard
a man is seen hanging
from a rope
the flesh of politics stapled
to his skin
Reagan turns and enters
his chambers
turns on the TV
there's a riot in the streets
and everyone looks like
Charlie Chaplin

the odor of death seeps through
the antenna as the Reagans
retire to bed
in the morning they wake
drink a glass of sake
and turn the TV back on

they are greeted by a string
of corpses walking backwards
into the walls
led by a midget carrying
the flag of Hiroshima
in his burned out eyes

REAGANITES

know nothing and preach all
reaganites cut the budget
to save us from the poor

reaganites hang out
with ex-Presidents
disbarred lawyers
and ex-cabinet members
carefully placing bets
on all possible probabilities

in times of high inflation
reaganites call upon
the poor to shoulder
the burden

in times of national emergencies
reaganites seek out masochists
hurting only those who like pain
and are able to pay for it

reaganites do not favor
the rich
they are the rich

reaganites are not concerned
with money
they print it

reaganites interpret dreams
as Un-American

reaganites eat apple pie
on Mother's Day

and pray to the Easter Bunny
for deliverance.

reaganites espouse their philosophy
at barbershops, hot dog stands,
baseball games, picnics, american
legion events and the Super Bowl
but mostly at the Country Club
in between placing bets
on the lions against
the Christians

reaganites do not fear
the vote
they fix it

reaganites see the junta
as a legitimate means towards
re-educating the masses

reaganites raise children
so that Disneyland will become
a national shrine

reaganites cannot be brainwashed
only because they lack brains

reaganites invented herpes
to discourage sex

reaganites are against
the unemployed
but favor unemployment
as a necessary evil

reaganites like to make life safe
for democracy
and carry pictures of Judas
in their back pocket
and Marilyn Monroe
in their hearts

DIAL 890 REMEMBERING THE GOOD OLD SIXTIES

ladies and gentlemen
turn your dial to 890
on your favorite AM/FM
radio station
and see what is happening
in the Great Society

on the foreign scene
Vietnam peace talks stall
as the White House announces
it will move cautiously in dealing
with the Russians' latest move
toward Nuclear disarmament
because neither side can agree on
the proper date for talks to begin

in the meantime
Vietnam war continues
in the streets of Saigon while
negotiators quibble over
the size of the peace table
in beautiful downtown Paris

U.S. generals claim substantial
gains and important victories
in the past month while fresh supplies
of bodies are ordered by the Pentagon
for expected vacancies computed
to exist from statistical backlog
and Vietnam (Cong) terrorist activities

a massive assault on
the demilitarized zone gains fifty yards
into enemy territory with only

76 wounded
33 dead and
11 unaccounted for

Marine General commends his men
for bravery above and beyond the call of duty
while Da Nang reports
112 more wounded and
17 dead from enemy fire
on U.S. Air Force Base
said to be invincible by same
Marine general from his R and R area
in beautiful downtown Hong Kong

latest bulletin in from
Washington D.C. relates
the President in a special news bulletin
says things are not going well
in Paris and urges the people
to tighten their belts
and prepare for additional hardship
and possible larger war effort

U.S. mothers wired to give
their support in supplying more bodies
for further vacancies
to occur in the years ahead
fringe benefits said to include
a sense of serving the country
and a U.S. flag to drape
the government-financed casket
secured at no cost to the buyer
other than his life

FOR CHARLES OLCOTT

he'd been a computer engineer
and a good one
to judge his resume
but he'd been unemployed
for months
and he'd been despondent too
and yesterday they found the body
of Charles James Olcott
thirty-five beneath an oak tree
a plastic bag over his head
his resume, job application
and rejections nearby

Olcott father of three children
formerly owned his own business
and before that worked
for RCA Crocker Citizens Bank
Varian Associates and other firms
in the field of data systems
and programming

the search for employment
was discovered in papers scattered
nearby and in a small briefcase found
at his side

a graduate of San Francisco
State University with a major
in languages and extension courses
in computer engineering
at the University of California
at Berkeley

just last week
the President gave a talk

on the State of the Nation
and assured the folks
at the Commons Club
that 6% unemployment
was not necessarily unhealthy
for the economy
Charles James Olcott was not
among those found applauding

LIES

it's all a lie
nothing changes
the trees shed their leaves
like a burlesque dancer
the undertaker goes about
his business unceremoniously
the walls hide hidden messages
like greedy beggars
the doorbell rings
the telephone rings
nothing changes
it's all the same

the old man is thinking
of death
the young man is thinking
of riches
poets have become
exotic merchants of death

butterflies are beautiful
they have no desire
to fly to the moon
like Kaufman said:
"poets don't sneak
into zoos and talk
to tigers anymore"

it's perfectly all right
to cast the first stone
if you have more than
the other person

the avon lady walks
on water

the blind man sniffing
his way up her leg
nothing changes
the wars go on
the lies go on
the boxing matches
the bullfights
the football games go on
and we go on too
like a tired tongue
resting between the legs
of a bored woman

the truth is that
d.a. levy was right
"sum people just cannot
beat the system"
and poets can't even pretend
they are beating the system

DURING THE DEBATE BETWEEN CLINTON AND DOLE

I was in the Mission
with the hookers dopers
and the homeless
none of whom were watching
the debate

during the sparring and jabbing
the police seemed disinterested
not having time for donuts
at the 18th street coffee shop
eyeing suspiciously the alcoholics
the disabled Vietnam Vet
with one leg limping
his way to nowhere

the furniture store with
a TV in the display window
drew no one but a single
transvestite who may have been
sizing up the candidates
but not for their political positions

I got in my car and drove
to the Tenderloin
on the other side of town
where a topless dancer
had the attention
of two blue-suited businessmen
with eyes hungry
as a German Shepherd dog
tongues panting for a piece
of paradise
the bored bartender fighting
off sleep watching the woman

dance on the raised stage
with neon lights flashing
just outside the bar door
the poor the hungry
the lonely embracing
as the two candidates
argued on the merits
of western civilization

THEY'RE AT IT AGAIN

they say they want to clean up
the tenderloin
going after the massage parlors
and prostitutes
in their annual crackdown
on sin charade
when the real sin is the homeless
battered women and children
gay bashing and wall street criminals
perjury and the destruction of justice
by bought and paid for politicians

It's all status quo—business as usual
as we hire more cops
to protect business interests
tear gas peaceful protestors
build more prisons
to discourage revolution
while cutting back on food stamps
for the poor and school breakfasts
for over 40,000 children
in order to give the richest
of the rich another tax break

the finest minds of our generation
enslaved in university classrooms
or working in scientific labs creating
new weapons of mass destruction
the hungry jaws of capitalism
chewing on the flesh of the poor
and institutionalizing the elderly
but not before squeezing every
last drop of blood from
the working class man and woman

the young dance like puppets
on a string
in a Disneyland production
Fox News presenting
their "balanced" news:
in an unbalanced way
as our elected officials
primp in front of mirrors
like cocky peacocks preparing
to destroy timberland and rain forests
in payment for political contributions
as they enact voter suppression laws
to keep the status quo alive another
two thousand years

CHINATOWN SWEAT SHOP

you see them coming
but never going working
fourteen sixteen-hour shifts
six seven days a week

I imagine the sewing machine
humming, "a stitch in time saves nine."

you see them coming
but never going
the madam's eyes
an executioner in disguise
watching waiting as the system
grinds them into oblivion

FACTORY WORKER

he toils on the assembly line
works an eight ten hour shift
leaves a piece of him behind
for every part he helps make

at night at home
he hides his thoughts
like smuggled contraband
sewn inside the false compartment
of a suitcase

he wears jeans made
in Honduras
shoes made in Mexico
a shirt from Korea
a hat from China

makes love to his wife
brought over from Russia
with ruble eyes
and milky white thighs
that mask the capitalistic lies

LOSS OF INNOCENCE

I lost whatever innocence
I had back in '68
Robert Kennedy murdered
Mai Lai a month later
the Chicago 7
storm troopers wielding clubs
like cavemen of old
Richard Nixon signaling
the beginning of the end
those eyes
those wide eyes digging
holes in my heart
napalm fire kissing that
child's innocent body
black smoke hugging her skin
as television pundits played
their spin
this war that we could never
win

ON THE BOMBING OF YUGOSLAVIA

it's history repeating itself
all over again
from Napoleon
to Attila the Hun
gothic nightmares
slaughterhouse mentality
old glory versus fascism
genocide versus annihilation
war criminals posing
as heads of state
masturbating messiahs
wearing the masks of Hiroshima
and Auschwitz
the bones of women and children
fuel for Hitler's ovens
played out once again
in Kosovo while corporate
America stands guard
at Fort Knox

I WILL NOT PLEDGE ALLEGIANCE

I will not pledge allegiance
to the flag of the U.S.
and all it has come
not to stand for
I will not bow down
to corporate America
and its religious right
I will not cannot accept
your moral bankruptcy
your greenback God buying
and selling lives
on the stock market exchange

I will not bow down to a country where
assassins determine the course of history
whose papal church has its own bank
where ka-ching ka-ching has become
the new holy mantra

J. Edgar Hoover died
in order to go to heaven
and tap the private line of God
secretly monitoring Jesus' every move

America
you have become
one big insane asylum
your manic-depressive innkeepers
waging war on the masses
your henchmen standing proud
on your purple majestic mountains
kissing the cold stone faces
on Mount Rushmore
looking like a mafia don with
the cold kiss of death
on his breath

WE THE PEOPLE

we keep on voting these assholes
into office
then complain like a nagging wife
or we don't vote at all which means
the biggest asshole gets elected
the one who raises the most money
the one who sells his favors
the one with a Harvard accountant
who otherwise would have been working
for the Mafia

and they campaign on promises
they have no intention of keeping
or prostitute them if they do
these men with billboard smiles
and sweaty palms
these men of chauffeured limousines
and Lysol clean toilets
with a daughter on the honor roll
and a son with no honor
at all

BILL

he keeps a photograph tucked
inside his meager belongings
three smiling soldiers
smoking cigarettes
a Viet Cong in black pajamas
hanging upside down
from a pole
gutted like a fish
flesh nailed to Jesus like cross
needs no caption

guilt shadows him in doorways
and under freeways where
he makes his home

incoming artillery tears
at his nerves
pieces of flesh stuck
to bamboo
like a piece of meat thrust
into a tiger's cage

Vietnamese peasants
suspected Cong haunt
his dreams like
a faceless Santa Claus
leaving behind a bag
of body parts under
a scorched Christmas tree

OLD JOE

he sleeps in doorways
or on park benches
doesn't want to go
to a shelter
not even when prodded
with the heavy weight
of the cop's nightstick

under threat of jail
he curls up in a fetal position
and closes his eyes trying
to shut out memories of Vietnam
nightmares that whirl inside
his head like helicopter blades

the alcohol the drugs
the failed years gather
like locusts inside
the cranial guitar of his mind
play all night rhapsodies inside
his head

warrior troubadour of Pharaoh origins
pale spokesman of lost tribes
masked as a homeless transient
poet prophet of beauty
and all its imperfections
ravished by the streets
kissed by angels
left tired withered like
a neglected Kansas grain field

FOLSOM PRISON

at Folsom Prison
the guards joke
and laugh as they have me empty
my pockets inside out
take everything from me
leave me with only a notebook
and a handful of poems

the guard in the watchtower
eyes the prisoners
in the courtyard below
his high-powered rifle
at the ready

the warden distrustful
perhaps even fearful stations
a guard outside the small room
where the poetry workshop is held

the sharing of words
barely begins when
I look outside the window
see a bird on top of the prison wall
looking east then west before
spreading its wings and flying north
free as a bird was meant to be
as I turn my attention
to the guard stationed in the back
of the room
hiding behind dark shades
looking more the outlaw than
the law

SAN QUENTIN PRISON

the tower guard surveys
the courtyard below
gun at the ready
here in the museum
of the living dead

night shadows gather
dark as a tattoo
prisoners arrive steady
as labor pains
brought to their knees
by men with steel tip boots
black as tar
with eyes that search
the cellblock
like a hungry wolf
in search of fresh meat

UNTITLED

McDonald's wrappers
mating with Coca-Cola cans
float across the rivers of America
Walt Whitman's children
forced to inhale exhaust fumes
each breath coated in death

Christ run out of town
for practicing his trade without
a union card
children weaned
on Campbell's chicken noodle soup
unaware of all those tiny booger
hearts floating in a sea of fat

POEM FOR HIS HOLINESS

priests dressed in robes
of splendor
the Vatican with its own bank
one hundred poor boys
in the drunk tank
tv evangelists shacking up
with whores
priests molesting young boys
tossed into the dung heap
like kindling wood
a blanket of human bones
to keep the church fires burning

SITTING BULL

poet of the plains
forced to ride across
the range
the face of the white man
waiting in ambush

sitting bull
poet of earth and water
you fought the white man's army
to a stand-still
only to find yourself Buffalo Bill's
sidekick
sentenced to kill Custer over
and over again
to the cheers of wild west crowds

from horses buffalo and ponies
to a black exhaust fume car
you rode the wave of despair
forever branded
with the white man's scars

POEM FOR THE GOVERNOR OF ARIZONA

they cross the border
looking for a piece
of the promised land
entering a country that once
belonged to their ancestors
these conquered souls
of Mexico
who toil in fields of abundance
harvesting fruit and vegetable
with stooped backs
and blistered hands
at pay no white man would consider
in a land built by immigrants
it now considers its enemy

222 EDDY STREET

she sits alone
in her hotel room
above the 222 Club
at Ellis and Eddy street
pregnant, forced to give
head, for soup and bread

hope bled dry
immigrant without visa
or stature
an illegal caught
in a legal trap

feels the baby stir
move inside her
lead belly blues plays
downstairs in tavern

she heads for the door
hears the night manager whisper whore
suspended in silence and grief
floats face down in the bowels
of the american dream

4 A.M. INSOMNIA POEM

lost in the never
never land of insomnia
a dark forest ravished by storms
where dreams go to perish

my mind hijacks my destiny
speaks in tongues
devours the silence
walks hunchbacked
like a gypsy tailor
pushing a garment cart

a sacrificial virgin burns
in volcanic ash
a Tijuana Jesus
nailed to a plastic cross
winks at the twelve wise men
making a return trip to the manager
after a shopping spree at Waymart's

a fortune teller trades in
her crystal ball
for a pack of tarot cards
the lone survivor of a shipwreck
float aimlessly at sea
my love returns from
the Bermuda Triangle
in the disguise of a mermaid
a bee colony drips honey between
the legs of a Dairy Queen
a haunted house coughs up
an angry ghost drunk on death

Dante gives up his seat in hell
to Rosa Parks
who recites the lord's prayer
backwards to a honky sheriff
in Selma, Alabama

the FDA declares sleeping masks
a fraud
Van Gogh demands his ear back
a new born baby is sacrificed
at the Louvre
a French mistress closes her legs
in protest

the mirror mocks my image
two decades of sleeplessness
camp inside my skull
hot as volcano ash
Satan stops by to recruit me
God makes no counter offer
a whisper of sleep camps inside
my eyeballs
I surrender with a whimper
drown in a series
of Hail Mary's
recited by sexy nuns
in see-through attire

SAN FRANCISCO BLUES

Iran, Iraq, Libya
Africa, ethnic cleansing
Bill Gates, Donald Trump
and the Pope
all selling their own brand
of dope

a mayor who is a joke
a bus system that doesn't work
head cases walking the street
punk rockers with rainbow hair
women with pierced genitals
ginseng for tired blood

my illusions are fighting
a duel with my delusions
the last time I picked up
a white courtesy telephone
the voice on the other end
was mine

the dates on my calendar
are blank
the pinball machine
has no flappers
there's no prize
in my crackerjack box
my radio plays nothing
but commercials
my hand holds my cock
in contempt
my love life is an unread resume
with one too many references

I had a dream
I was a gunrunner trading
hardware for software
I want my photo on a cereal box
not a milk carton

the IRS is a legal shake down
the Pentagon a slaughterhouse
Jack the Ripper sliced
and diced his way through
London Town
and he wasn't even a chef

Freud was impotent
but put on a good show
Monks know the truth
but won't share it
you know you're in trouble
when your shrink deals
in fantasies and leaves you
with his reality

my life has become
a distraction
no additions and subtractions
when it becomes an abstraction
I'll know I've found success

LOOKING FOR AN ANSWER

I went to a poetry reading
not long ago
only the second time
in several years
to see if things had changed
and they hadn't

the first reader was
a middle class female poet
who teaches at a university
and knocks down
$40,000 a year
who read about the homeless
the dispossessed and the bombing
of the World Trade Center
and other things she knew little
if anything about
and the audience ate it up
and clapped like sea lions
in a mating ritual
soon to be followed by a male poet
who was the exact opposite
an apparent hold over
from the sixties
dressed in army fatigues
with long hair down
to his shoulders
who spoke about the same things
in a slightly more indignant
tone of voice
here at a coffee house café
just three blocks from
Mission Street
the home of prostitutes
and the homeless
and the crowd ate it up some more

and I kept thinking
we're so full of ourselves using
words as a preaching tool
while all around us
people are starving and dying
and committing genocide while
we stand up on stage
eager for applause
or send our work out to the zines
seeking elusive recognition
for reasons even we don't know
playing to the audience
telling the most intimate secrets
of our lives
pretending to be knowledgeable
when in reality we know so little
trying to make the big poetry
grand slam
trying to make the top ten
unlike the music industry where
there's room for the top forty

like the poet Bob Kaufman said
"poets don't sneak into zoos
and talk to tigers anymore."

rams out fucking sheep
poets playing trick-or-treat
politicians beating their meat
whores making it under
the sheets
homosexuals lined-up
with elbow grease
landlords waiting to cancel
your lease
it's got so bad that

you can't tell the real ones
from the elite
everyone has become
a carbon copy of themselves

take a number
step up on stage
rattle the cage
let loose your rage
don't forget your cell
the call you miss
may be from god

stand tall stand proud
work the crowd
like a carnie hustler
send your resume
to poets and writers
fax the late night show
it's the way to go
bro

and when the reading was over
all that was missing was
the exchanging of high-fives
and I had to ask myself
what was I doing there
when I could have been home
watching Michael Jordan
and the Chicago Bulls
school the crowd on what
life is really all about

ON WHY I WRITE POLITICAL POEMS

friends keep chiding me
for writing political poems while
spending their own time mimicking
a reality tv show
sort of like smoking marijuana
and not inhaling
if you know what I mean

I honestly don't know
I've thought of going
to the mountains where
it's legal to tote a gun
or maybe move to Vegas
and become a legal gangster
either way it's a death warrant
and since I don't have any real family
I've sort of adopted the dispossessed
for my own
and it's the downtrodden
who get fucked by the politicians
like newt gingrich said
let's hire children in the schools
and put them to work mopping floors
and cleaning toilets

and maybe this is why when
I was depressed with a serious
neck injury, I fought
to save myself, knowing
god wasn't up to the task
so here I am in the twilight years
still fighting the system
still fighting myself
Nietzsche inside my head
Hemingway in my blood seconds before

he pulled the trigger
and wasn't it Mao who said
"after the revolution the poets must be
the first to go?"
but he couldn't have been talking about
the Beats Ginsberg and Burroughs
having done commercials
and Dylan selling the rights
to "The Times They Are A-Changin"
to corporate america
when does the high road become
the low road?
no amount of words
can raise the dead
and death knows no remorse
takes no holidays
better that I write these words
than write a grant request
to the NEA
better I protest rather than ride
the poetry circuit pony
better that I be true to myself
than sell out for a lottery chance
at fame

POEM FOR ALLEN GINSBERG

I saw the best minds of my generation
destroyed by greed
naked under their fashion
designer clothes
driving themselves through congested
city streets
looking for free parking spaces
aging hormone driven
biological clock mothers offering
in public their purple veined breasts
to baby suckling zombies
who stock market driven sipped
Starbucks coffee while chatting
aimlessly on their cell phones
making reservations at trendy
restaurants while whining about
the quality of the wine
who shopped at organic food markets
looking for eternal youth
and fucked only by appointment
who saw the savior while vacationing
in Palm Springs
and God on Turner TV
who taught their children
how to use ATM machines
while devising tax fraud schemes
who drove their cars
in the bicycle lane hoping
for some excitement
who pierced their nipples cocks
and tongues
wanting to be among
the hip and young
who pledged allegiance
to the almighty dollar while

writing protest letters
to their daily newspaper

holy is the sock
holy is swiss cheese
holy is the ATM machine
holy is cable TV

holy is the condom
holy is the U.N.
holy is pop culture
holy is Bank of America
Ka-ching
        Ka-ching
                Ka-ching
the new holy order
the holy of the unholy
the best minds
of my generation

HOSPITAL POEM

so many hospitals with
so many names
of so many saints
it makes the heart want
to bleed
Saint Francis Saint Mary
Saint Joseph and Saint Luke's
Saint this one and Saint that one
so many people lined up waiting
to die
hacking coughing spitting-
up their insides

so many nurses
with dollar bill eyes
strutting their stuff into
the parking lots
into the nearby bars
too tired to make conversation
too tired to make love

so many doctors
so sad they can't be God
they hide their failures between
the legs of the angels of mercy
so frustrated they take out
their anger on the golf courses
of America

so many cardiac arrests
so many dead on arrival
so many Jane Doe's
so many John Doe's
how many no one knows
and the security guards

and the housekeeping staff
and the accountants
and the gray haired lady volunteers
with eyes worn as a buffalo head nickel

so many lonely people
so many sad faces
so many bodies removed
by grim faced undertakers
who see death as morning cereal
while you and I wait
on the inevitable
like a long line of gamblers
at the race track

and some go whimpering
and some go yelling
and some go without
saying a word
some go like Joe Louis
or Ted Williams champs
to the end
and some go out like Ali
stuttering stammering
just trying to see it through
another day

and life goes on as it should
and must
with budgets to be cut
halls to be scrubbed
twenty-year service pins
for the survivors
and the nurses so young
with their orange blossom smell

walk it by your door and my door
lacking love lacking grace lacking pity
worn down beat upon
they eat they sleep
they masturbate
with hands and vibrators
some none too cleverly
some like Van Gogh
walking the halls like
vampires with painted fingernails
that slice the flesh
to the bone

the doctors the nurses
the orderlies in white
the priests
the patients the relatives
and loved ones
all seeking a private audience
with God
here behind these sterile walls
where death stalks the halls
with panting breath licking
the crevice of the soul

death the noble savage
death the avenging sadist
leaving behind her scars
playing out the game
to the bitter end
a giant hearse among
a sea of compact cars

THE OLD POETS

the old poets don't read anymore
they are content to scan
the pages of major literary journals
looking for their names in print
their books reviewed
the old poets borrow lines
from their contemporaries
but only when suffering writer's block
the old poets no longer have mother
Russia to comfort them
the old poets have no party to join
no Red Guard to march with
no parades to goose-step too
the old poets sprinkle wheat germ
on their cereal and drink bottled water
the old poets forsake salt with meals
take pride in the little known fact
an average spill of semen contains
less than twenty-five calories
the old poets have no causes
left to die for
no homeland to call their own
the old poets have turned in
their bombs and union cards
for small change
and social security
the old poets are tired
like Atlas they have learned
the hard way you can't carry
the world on your shoulders
the old poets have traded in
their party cards for government grants
the old poets realize that suffering
is overrated
the old poets have quit writing

political poems
no longer carry Nietzsche inside
their hearts
the old poets ride
the poetry circuit pony express
grabbing at the gold ring
all too willing to sell themselves
for a lottery chance
at fame

THE SHOW MUST GO ON

The following poem was composed from various newspaper accounts over the years of Executions and the argument for and against Capital Punishment. Ecstatic Peace Press previously published The Show Must Go On in a longer version as a chapbook.

this is not a poem about
Ted Bundy
well not exactly
though history will record
that at precisely 7:16
on the morning
of January 15, 1988
Ted Bundy made his final peace
if mass killers can ever be said
to find inner peace

after a night of crying
and praying
Bundy was strapped
into the death chamber
to be executed for his sins

one has to wonder
what went on inside his head
as they strapped his chest
arms and legs to the wooden chair
his eyes searching the window
for signs of a familiar face
seeming to nod at those
he recognized including the man
who had prosecuted him
as his lips moved in a faint smile
making one wonder what
he was thinking those last moments
with his head bowed as if in meditation
his skull glistening where an ointment

had been applied to enhance
the work of the electrodes.

when asked if he had any last words
Bundy hesitated and said
in a slightly quivering voice:
"Give my love
To my family and friends."

with these last words
the guards pulled a thick strap
across his mouth and chin bolting
the metal skullcap into place
its heavy black veil
falling over his face

and with a prearranged signal
an anonymous State Executioner
wearing a hood to hide his identity
pushed the button sending
two thousand volts of electricity
surging through the wires causing
his body to tense into a clench
as a tiny puff of smoke
lifted from one leg

a minute or so later
which must have seemed
like an eternity
a paramedic opened Bundy's
blue prison shirt and listened
for a heart beat while
a doctor aimed a small light into
his eyes
at 7:16 a.m.

Theodore Robert Bundy
was officially pronounced dead
but the real story lay across
the dewy grass of a cow pasture
where five hundred people
had gathered to cheer the execution

when word came that
Ted Bundy was dead
the mass of humanity began chanting
BURN BUNDY BURN
while others sang or hugged or banged
on frying pans they had brought
for the occasion
it was clear for the moment
that everyone was having a good time
and that society had extracted
its just due
but then this isn't a poem about
Ted Bundy
well not exactly
for history will record
that as a civilized nation
we have burned people chained
them up to starve
or to be eaten by vultures
stoned them castrated them gutted them
torn them into pieces
and even crucified them
and history tells us
that one man in New Orleans
was nailed into a wooden box
and sawed in half
and hanging is still a favorite

sport in many states
perhaps a hold over from
the good old frontier days
and the state of Utah offers
the option of a firing squad
so it was only natural as time passed
that an inventive man would come along
to invent the electric chair
which was sold
as a more kindly state of death
only Rubert Webber the first man
to be executed in it
might have disagreed
it being reported Rubert refused
to die quietly or quickly
the first 2000 volts of electricity
merely singing his skin
so being humane as Americans are
along came Hap Travis from Eaton
Metal Works in Denver
to develop the patent
to the gas chamber
Aaron Mitchell
a poor black man from
Mississippi would be
the first to test its efficiency
dragged screaming from his cell
One April morning in 1967
so mad with fear that he slashed
his arm with a razor blade
and spent his last 24 hours
standing naked in a crucified
position proclaiming himself
to be the Second Coming of Christ

now I mean that's what
you call putting on a real show
and we'll never know if Lenderess Riley
found it humane or not
what history does record is that he too
was dragged to the gas chamber
screaming and filled with terror
much like Aaron Mitchell before him

and in the first recorded case
of female equality
Barbara Graham became
the first woman put to death
by the State of California

it's said a prison guard told her
death would come easier
if she took a deep breath
and slowly counted to ten
to which it is said she replied
"how in the hell would you know?"

the fact that many people
even today consider her innocent
of the crime for which she was convicted
did not keep the show from going on
but being the humane race we are
we keep improving on the methods until
today lethal injection has become
the popular means for legalized murder
despite the fact that in Texas
it took a half-hour to find
the vein of a junkie who didn't
die quickly at all

and in another recorded case
of a messy execution
it took more than an hour before
the victim died
so messy was the execution
the authorities had to pull
the curtain of the viewing room
so as not to make the witnesses sick
and the state of Florida took pride
in "Old Smoky"
(A three-legged oaken seat)
built by prisoners at Florida
State Prison in 1923)
to administer the tried and true
two thousand volt current applied
to 225 convicted criminals

the most memorable taking place
in March 1997
to dispatch Pedro Medina
a 39-year-old Cuban immigrant
to his maker

Pedro was strapped into the chair
at 7:10 a.m. and what happened
after this is public record
as something went terribly wrong
with flames leaping from
the masked head of the convicted murderer
so much smoke filling the death chamber
that an outside window had to be opened
not that this was Florida's
first botched execution
Old Smoky had to be unplugged

for several months in 1990 after
smoke and flames were seen near the head
of another convicted murderer during
an excruciating electrocution
in which three jolts of current
were administered over
a four-minute period

Florida officials said his death
was quicker even if more spectacular
which seems at odds with
the State Attorney General
who said shortly after the execution:
"People who commit murder
had better not do it in Florida
because we may have a problem
with our electric chair"
this from an elected official
of a State that can't even
get its voting machines to work right
and an enlightened Florida lawmaker
twenty-four hours later
introduced legislation suggesting
the guillotine as a more humane
method of execution
and the state of Utah perhaps
not wanting to be out done offers
a menu with a wide variety of choices:
the electric chair the gas chamber
lethal injection or a firing squad
the debate on whether
capital punishment is a deterrent
has been going on for over a century
and a Tufts University study purports
that a fair-sized number of Californians

were convicted of murders they didn't commit
lucky enough to be vindicated
luckier still to have lived long enough
to be vindicated before their death
sentence was carried out
but it took from one to twenty-five years
to win their freedom though
we hear little if anything about such things
unless in rare instances
a condemned man comes from privileged class

and the Governor of the state
of Illinois suspended all executions
after it was revealed a number
of condemned men had been wrongly
sentenced to die
but in Texas they boast the highest
capital death rate in the nation

and history tells us in
the 19th Century in England
they had public hangings
to discourage pick-pocketing
only to find this crime increased
during the hangings which would
seem to lend credence
to those who claim
Capital Punishment does not
deter crime.

and in a poll of 84% of expert Criminologists
from the U.S.
it was concluded that the death penalty
is not a deterrent
and it's a documented fact

we have a significantly
higher murder rate
than in countries like
Europe that do not have
the death penalty

and never mind the fact
The American Bar Association states
those who murdered whites were found
to be remarkably more likely
to be sentenced to death
than those who murder people of color
seemingly undisputable evidence
of racial disparity in the application
of the death penalty

so the politicians and blood lust crowd
have turned to cost as an arguing factor
but in the leading execution State of Texas
it has been estimated the cost
of one death costs on average
$2.32 million dollars
three times the cost of imprisoning
a person in a single
high security cell for over
forty years

but public executions have been
public sport ever since
the Romans introduced the Christians
to the lions or Pontius Pilot gave in
to the mob so it's not surprising
the government and the courts invited
the families of the victims
of the Oklahoma bombing to watch

the execution of Timothy McVeigh
on closed circuit TV
and though no tickets were sold to the event
you can be sure there was a good time had
for those who haven't forgotten
The Ted Bundy Show
for like they say in Hollywood
the Show must go on

POEM FOR A POET FRIEND

I know this poet who plays
the poetry-biz game
he knows how to trade favors
in twenty-four assorted flavors
his days pass faster than
the muteness of his message
he could have been
a stand-up comedian
a burlesque dancer had
he been born a woman
this master weaver spinning tales
like Jerry Lewis courting
Abbot and Costello

seriousness is being treated
like a sickness
a cancer to be avoided
at all costs
its grand slams and elite
poetry festivals
run by grand marshals
and their elves
the wasteland of blurred visions
lies like an idle land mine
waiting to explode
in the minds of circus clowns

these poets have become wizards
of attack
to them a crisis
is a loose bowel movement
a skipped heartbeat or two
but what of the crisis
of the social system
a system of calculated murder

a system of chemical
and environmental cancer
a system of the poor and elderly
a system of sadness
how do I laugh about this
how do I laugh about
my brothers in prison
my dead comrades racing across
bloodstained clouds
their bruised feet bringing down
hard rain
a rain that does not cleanse
but leaves behind scars
and torn flesh
and still the games go on
red poets who write love poems
for Stalin
populist poets turned businessmen
who hang out at Spec's and
the Café Trieste
courting the favors of the NEA
and campaigning to be
the next city poet laureate

I can't wear the easy grin
it's an ill-fitting suit
my mind a tailor who fits
me with needled threads
and yes there is a place for laughter
and I too can pen a funny line
but poetry is more than laughter
more than stepping up on stage
one hand on the poem
the other on the applause meter
and it was a Russian poet

who said the function of poetry
must be to make us blush
with shame
and it was an American poet
who said "the dams reverse
themselves and want
to go stand alone in the desert."
this is why these poems are sad
the long dead running over
the fields
the masses sinking down
the light in the children's faces
fading at six or seven

these are the voices I heed
knowing the poet must believe
in what he says and writes
that a poet's responsibility
goes beyond the written word

a poet must be angry
but he must be able
to sing too
his words must melt like honey
on a blistered tongue
for flat-backed whales sing
and birds sing
but my poet friend has forgotten
how to sing
it shows in his eyes
it shows in his nervous laughter
it shows in his words on the page

my poet friend writes
a poem a day

he spends his time in coffee houses
and courts the favors of those in power
he does not visit the jails
the prisons the forests
the bowery
the freezing North Dakota dawn
he does not feel the whisper
of the secret that passes over
the plains

DANCING WITH WORDS

there are poets who like
to dance with words
but dancing for an audience
isn't like moving
to the music on your own
stirring the notes of the soul

there are poets who organize
festivals and such
poets who live for applause
poets who divide through elitism
poets who attack the system
but live off it

fame kills
Billie Holiday's ghost attests
to this
money pigeonholes
power corrupts
the spiritual truth
the scriptures tell us this
the true poet knows this
stands tall above
the dancing with word poets
who are little more
than instruments of a poem
greater than themselves

be like Li Po and sail your poems
on streams and puddles written
on leaves
the voice of and for the people
risk your life your literary life
for the dispossessed who need

your voice in desperate times
live among them inspire them
love them become one with them

this is the mark of the true poet
the poetry-biz boys are not poets
Walt Whitman is an example
of what poetry is
who stood tall and fearless against
his enemy
which is never really man
but the poison in his soul:
pride envy and lust
how can those afflicted with
the disease of egomania
jealousy and desire for fame
write about and from the heart

gone is the fire of Whitman
and Baudelaire
one column of media praise
is of less value than
a single teardrop on a poem
from a waitress in a greasy diner
these people know nothing of genius
how can cockroaches evaluate eagles?
the true poet's topic is people
not the poet

FOURTH OF JULY POEM

stepped on pissed on cheated
and abused, taken advantage
of blue collar man, caught up
in the American scam
don't tell me anyone
can be anything they want to be
if they put their minds to it
your message won't sell in Harlem
or to the West Virginia coal miners
or the immigrants
you have turned your back on

   take your message to the church
   tell it to the men on death row
   tell it to the starving poor
   tell it to the sick and lame
   tell it to the politicians
   tell it to the serial killers
   tell it to the bankers
   tell it to Wall Street
   tell it to the union busters
   tell it to the man on the gallows
   tell it to the cowardly terrorists
   tell it to the last man at the Alamo
   tell it to Madonna
   tell it to the street whore
   tell it to the last wino
   on the bowery
   tell it to the butcher
   tell it to the unemployed
   tell it to the circus clown
   tell it to the insane
   tell it to the outlaw
   tell it to the in-laws
   tell it to the panhandler

tell it to the conman
tell it to the displaced
factory worker
tell it to the elderly
tell it to the re-po man
tell it to the last space alien
hiding out in Roswell
tell it to the militia
tell it to the FBI sharpshooters
at Ruby Ridge
tell it to the arsonists
at Waco, Texas
tell it to the junkie with dry heaves
tell it to the farm worker
tell it to the dishwasher
tell it to the orderlies
tell it to the flag waver
tell it to the garment worker
slaving away in sweat shops
in Chinatown
and the Latin Quarter
tell it to the garbage man
tell it to big business
tell it to the oil barons
tell it to the tobacco merchants
tell it to the children addicted
to tv and video games
tell it to the molested children
tell it to the battered wives of America
tell it to the pharmacy industry
dispensing billions of dollars
of drugs each year
tell it to the millions of people
dying from air pollution
in China and Mexico

tell it to the man on his deathbed
not sure why he lived
or what he is dying for
tell it to Jesus Christ
shout it to the stars
line the traitors up against the wall
rewrite the Ten Commandments
and start all over again

POEM FOR ROBERTO VARGAS AND THE NICARAGUAN FREEDOM FIGHTERS

this poem is for you Roberto
and for Ed "Foots" Lipman too
this poem is for every poet
who ever paced the cellblocks of San Quentin,
Folsom, Attica, and Neil Island
or fought the people's struggle in Chile
Cuba or Nicaragua

this poem is for those who walk
the dream of freedom
with guerilla visions
in their hearts and eyes

this poem is for those
who gave their lifeblood
to wash the streets free of oppression
for those who rest in heroic
and not so heroic graves
in the struggle for human dignity

I sit here in my seventy-fifth year
thinking of young boys
who have fought the real war
of grieving mothers and widows
thinking of young girls with color-book eyes
young women in black suspender belts
and knee-high leather boots
with revolutionary roots

thinking of how the words come too late
and never say enough
knowing that in the Buddha Temple of life
all things must die
knowing there is no survival

no tarot cards horoscopes or incantations
to bring back the dead.

I walk the midnight supermarket of death
thinking of Lorca and that long dirt road
thinking of the execution wall
the hangman's noose
ethnic cleansing ovens
and genocide
hearing the gypsy ballad
that sings to the heavens
knowing there is a strange code
to this language
we are addicted to
as Gene Fowler pointed out
evil spelled backwards is live
being made into a State
automated robot is evil
but dying is not evil
for it is in its whole
the disintegration
the bacterial feeding which
in turn is a live process
and so the fight goes on
and must go on until every street
has been cleared of assassins
until every newborn
is encircled in a poem
the spirit living on
in those passed the baton

the vision cannot be killed
even as we retreat into
the depths of our being
listening to the blood

beat solid against the walls
of the heart knowing
there are secrets in the bones
that cannot be denied
or sold out to the whims
of others

sleep well my comrades
only the flesh is gone
your strength lives on
in those who dared
to reach out and kiss
the sun

I AM SAN FRANCISCO

I have witnessed the waterfront decay
the ships disappear
the piers given over to tourists
and sunbathing sea lions

Gone the Haight Theater
in the old Haight Ashbury
where as a kid I paid a dime to see
two movies a serial and a newsreel

Gone the old Embassy Theater
on Market Street where
they spun the Wheel of Fortune
playing Ten-o-Win
with a busty female usherette shouting
"In the Balcony 1-2-3-4 Silver Dollars"
her breasts bouncing in unison
with each coin that hit the tray

The old Fox and Paramount Theaters
now ghostly memories
the old Market Street porno house
boarded down
McFarland's Fudge Shop
and Merrill's Drug Store gone

Gone the old Hoffbrau house
on Market Street
Breen's on Third Street
with the world's best Martini

Gone I. Magnum's Department Store
and the old City of Paris
where as a child I thrilled
at the sight of the giant Christmas tree

and who can forget The Emporium
its indoor ice-skating rink
and a Santa Claus workshop
the roof top garden where
rides included a Ferris wheel
a small roller coaster
and a train for children to ride

Gone the North Beach Beat hangouts:
The Place The Co-existence Bagel Shop
and the old Coffee Gallery where
Janice Joplin sang as an unknown
gone the old Barbary Coast where
as a teenager I tried to sneak into a bar
to catch a glimpse of a naked female dancer
long before Carol Doda
and topless and bottomless bars

Lenny Bruce and the old Purple Onion
fading memories like
Play Land at the beach
and the old burlesque house
in the Mission
gone the way of trolley car tokens
Fleer's Double Bubble Gum
and the Sutro baths

Third and Howard Street
the old skid row given a face-lift
the new skid row between
Sixth and Seventh Streets
home to drug dealers and alcoholics
an open festering wound
the city fathers ignore

Martini's now an old people's drink
Whiskey Sours just a memory
the Waterfront dives that served
Seamen and Long Shore men replaced
by new movie complexes and parking lots

The Mission once home of the Irish
has gone Latino
North Beach is moving
from Italian to Asian

The Greeks long ago moved to Burlingame
and no one knows what happened
to the American Indian
and the bar they frequented
on Valencia Street
and yet the city remains a magical
living breathing theater
of eccentric characters
that go back to Emperor Norton

You can still get a reasonably priced drink
at the 3300 Club in the Mission
or if you can afford it
go to the Top of the Mark
for a $13 hot chocolate drink with
a shot of Stolly Vodka and Southern Comfort
and enjoy one of the most beautiful views
in the world
or on a hot summer afternoon enjoy
an ice cream at Mitchell's on San Jose Avenue
where my father took the family
for an after dinner treat

You can still sun yourself
at Washington Square Park
watch young lovers lying on the grass
old men feeding pigeons
or walk the streets of Noe Valley
once a blue-collar neighborhood
now a Yuppie paradise
see young mothers with kids in strollers
eye women joggers
admire a dog sitting outside
Martha's Coffee Shop
faithfully waiting with pleading eyes
for table scraps from its owner

I am a Giants baseball fan
and a lifetime 49ers football addict
my heart still bleeds over the loss
of Seals Stadium and the old time
San Francisco Seals

I am the possessor
of framed achievement awards
and a baseball trophy from Panama where
I played a decent outfield

I am the only word-slinger
in a working class family
I am a ghost lost
in poetry books struggling to find
the right words to a hit song
like my idol Hank Williams

I am at war with my shadow
who shamelessly stalks me

I survived my apartment fire
to reestablish family ties
long buried in quicksand

my niece my nephew my great nephews
and great niece share my blood
a mixture of white and Mexican roots

my father's ghost walks my dreams
stares out the window of my soul
like he stared out the living room window
the year before his death.
my mother sitting at the dinner table
serving meat loaf and mashed potatoes
the air heavy as an anchor dragging
the ocean floor

I am San Francisco.

Also by A. D. Winans

Carmel Clowns (Atom Mind 1970)
Crazy John Poems (Grande Ronde 1972)
Straws Of Sanity (Thorpe Springs 1975)
Tales of Crazy John (Second Coming 1975)
North Beach Poems (Second Coming 1977)
ORG-1 (Scarecrow 1977)
All the Graffiti On All The Bathroom Walls Can't Hide These Scars Of Mine (Fallen Angel 1977)
The Further Adventures of Crazy John (Second Coming 1979)
The Reagan Psalms (Integrity Times Press 1984)
In Memoriam (Alpha Beat Press 1990)
A Knife In the Heart And Jazz In My Soul (Ancient Mariners 1996)
This Land Is Not My Land (Presa Press 1996)
The Charles Bukowski Second Coming Years (Beat Scene 1996)
Love Comes In Many Different Flavors (Ekskalibar 1996)
It Serves You Right To Suffer (Factotum 1996)
A Call To Poets (Green Bean Press 1997)
Venus In Pisces (Re-Presst 1997)
Remembering Jack Micheline (Red Cedar Press 1998)
America (Black Bear 1998)
Looking For An Answer (French Bread 1998)
San Francisco Streets (Yee Olde Font Shoppe 1998)
From Pussy To Politics (JVC 1999)
Folk Heroes & Other Strange Happenings (Benway Institute 1999)
Remembering Bukowski (Lummox 1999)
Scar Tissue (Lummox 1999)
People You think You Know (FourSep Press 1999)
Poems for the Poet, the Workingman, and the Downtrodden (Ibbetson Street 1999)
North Beach Revisited (Green Bean 2000)
13 Jazz Poems (X-Ray 2000)
City Blues (Editions Microbe 2001)
I Kiss The Feet Of Angels (Butcher Shop 2001)
The Holy Grail: Charles Bukowski And The Second Coming Revolution (Dustbooks 2002)
Whispers From Hell (Bottle of Smoke 2002)

Will the Real Lawrence Ferlinghetti Please Stand Up (12 Gauge 2002)
Trying To Find A Common Bond (Vojo Sindolic 2002)
A Bastard Child With No Place To Go (12 Gauge 2002)
The System (Centennial 2003)
A.D. Winans' Greatest Hits: 1995-2003 (Pudding House 2003)
Sleeping With Demons (Mystery Island 2003)
Whitman's Lost Children (24th Street Irregular Press 2004)
Dreams That Won't Leave Me Alone (Bottle Of Smoke Press 2004)
In Memoriam: New and Selected Poems (Chlensky Publishing 2004)
The Wrong Side Of Town (Cross Cultural Communications 2005)
This Land Is Not My Land (Presa Press 2005)
The Other Side Of Broadway: Selected Poems: 1965-2005 (Presa 2007)
The World's Last Rodeo (Bottle of Smoke 2006)
South of Market Street (Inequity Press 2006)
Marking Time (Erbacce 2008)
No Room For Buddha (Polymer Grove 2009)
Days In Heaven Nights In Hell (Propaganda Press 2009)
Billie Holiday Me And The Blues (Erbacce 2009)
Pigeon Feathers (Bottle Of Smoke Press 2009)
Dancing With Words (Propaganda Press 2010)
Love Minus Zero (Cross Cultural Communications 2010)
Black Lily (Rusty Truck Press 2010)
Drowning Like Li Po in a River of Red Wine:
    Selected Poems 1970-2010 (BOS Press 2010)
San Francisco Poems (Little Red Tree Publishing 2012)
Wind On His Wings (Presa Press 2012)
In the Dead Hours of Dawn (BOS Press 2012)
In the Pink (Pedestrian Press 2014)
Dead Lions (Punk Hostage Press 2014)

The New York Quarterly Foundation, Inc.
New York, New York

Poetry Magazine
Since 1969

Edgy, fresh, groundbreaking, eclectic—voices from all walks of life.

Definitely NOT your mama's poetry magazine!

The *New York Quarterly* has been defining the term contemporary American poetry since its first craft interview with W. H. Auden.

Interviews • Essays • and of course, lots of poems.

www.nyq.org

No contest! That's correct, NYQ Books are NO CONTEST to other small presses because we do not support ourselves through contests. Our books are carefully selected by invitation only, so you know that NYQ Books are produced with the same editorial integrity as the magazine that has brought you the most eclectic contemporary American poetry since 1969.

Books

www.nyq.org

poetry at the edge™

www.ingramcontent.com/pod-product-compliance
Lightning Source LLC
LaVergne TN
LVHW041340080426
835512LV00006B/544